Then *&* **Now**

CANTERBURY

The steam traction engine was the earliest form of mechanical power on the streets of Canterbury. This particular engine was owned and run by city hauliers G.F. Finn.

Then & Now
CANTERBURY

Compiled by
Paul Crampton

TEMPUS

Tempus Publishing Limited
The Mill, Brimscombe Port,
Stroud, Gloucestershire, GL5 2QG

ISBN 0 7524 1062 8

Typesetting and origination by
Tempus Publishing Limited
Printed in Great Britain by
Midway Clark Printing, Wiltshire

The modernist Longmarket under construction in 1960. The completed building can be seen on p. 86 and its bombed predecessor on p. 80.

Contents

Brett's prepare the ground for the construction of new shops on the south side of Burgate Street in February 1958. A picture of their predecessors is on p. 31.

Acknowledgements

I would like to thank Derek Butler, John Clark, Gerry Whittaker and Ted Yeoman for supplying photographic material. A special vote of thanks must also go to the photographers whose work appears herein. They are: Patrick Brown, David Cousins, Mr R.E. Cranfield, Bill Entwistle, Kenneth Gravett, Mr A Moody, Barrie Stretch, Dr William Urry, Rob Williams and Edward Wilmot.

My final word of appreciation goes to those who allowed me to use material from their archives: Barrett's of Canterbury, Canterbury Archeological Trust, Canterbury Local Study Collection, Canterbury Museums, English Heritage (RCHM) and the *Kentish Gazette*.

R1 class tank locomotive No. 31010 rests at Canterbury West Station having brought the last scheduled train from Whitstable on the old 'crab and winkle' line on 29 November 1952.

Introduction

A photograph freezes a moment in time that will never come again. As soon as the picture is taken, changes occur to the subject matter. Sometimes the changes are sudden and dramatic, such as when an individual old building is demolished or a loved one becomes ill. However, most changes wrought by the passage of time are slow and subtle, to the extent that most of us are unaware of them.

A good example is a typical shopping thoroughfare. Here, changes are piecemeal and spread over a period of time. One year, a trader and shop front might change, followed by the installation of new street lamps. Another year, properties might be modernized or even demolished, then pedestrianization introduced. Each successive year, the scene will gradually adapt to the needs of the traders and shoppers, as well as to those dictated by fashion and the current policy of the local authority.

This is where 'Then and Now' photography really comes into its own. All those changes are presented before you. Sometimes it will remind a long-standing resident of the way the street used to look; at other times it will show someone new to the area how the scene appeared in past times.

The value of 'Then and Now' pictures is not in the amount of time that separates them, but in the changes that are represented. Most of our towns and cities changed more in the 1950s and 1960s than at any other time, including the Blitz. Slum clearance, road widening and the shift from public to private transport have all left their mark.

Canterbury has seen more than its fair share of changes in the last hundred years. It was said that last century there was one pub in the city for every day of the year. In the early years of this century, many of these closed. Those that remained were modernized or, in some cases, completely rebuilt. Slum clearance began in the 1920s, escalated in the 1930s and after a short break (largely due to the effects of the Blitz) resumed in the late 1950s.

The Blitz itself obviously caused many unwelcome alterations to our city. But, more importantly, it provided a catalyst for even more changes, including a modernization plan which had already been planned to a large extent. Early post-war plans included the provision of a ring road and the widening of many existing roads. Conveniently, so-called slum housing was often the only thing in the path of these new or improved roads. Compulsory purchase often became a useful and cheap means of acquiring the necessary land (especially if the local health inspector could be persuaded to find some way to condemn the property as 'unfit for human habitation').

The needs of the ever increasing number of motor cars became even more demanding in the 1960s. New garages and filling stations appeared and existing facilities greatly expanded. Steam disappeared from our railways and goods sidings were ripped up as freight transport transferred to the roads. In the early 1970s, Canterbury's main street was pedestrianized. At the same time, many of the more useful shops which satisfied our daily needs, closed for good. Ultimately, they would be replaced by large supermarkets on the city's outskirts.

Currently, everyone is concerned about the environment. As a consequence, private cars are no longer welcome on our city streets. Intra-mural car park sites are being developed and park and ride sites are slowly appearing on the main trunk road approaches to Canterbury.

It would seem that buildings in modern styles are also no longer wanted in Canterbury. Many of these, including both good and bad examples, are currently being replaced by oversize developments in vernacular pastiche, leading to what some call the 'Disneyfication' of Canterbury!

Most of the changes that have occurred over the last 120 years are illustrated in the pages that follow. The old topographical photographs are accompanied by current shots taken from the same spot in the usual manner. However, this is more than just an ordinary 'Then and Now' book. For the first time, a number of social changes are represented. For example, we will see how we used to shop, get around and spend our leisure time. Consequently, the current or 'now' photographs will reflect how these things are done today and will therefore not necessarily be taken from the same location as the 'then' picture.

I have been passionately involved with Canterbury Then and Now photography for the last ten years, including my previous Meresborough series, Kentish Gazette features and Xarim Pictorial Books. I am very proud to include this Chalford Then and Now book amongst my finest achievements.

One
Main thoroughfares

The outer section of London Road in the 1890s, with large detached and semi-detached houses recently constructed on farmland either side. The road shows evidence of considerable use by horse-drawn traffic. Between the wars, electric lighting was installed and horses were gradually replaced by the internal combustion engine. In the late 1940s Temple Road was created between the two houses on the right to provide access to a new estate of prefabricated houses. In 1963, London Road was superseded by the A2 bypass, the Rheims Way. By this time, many of the houses had become small hotels or offices. Today, the trees of London Road are considerably more mature and the road is much busier.

Castle Street, part of the main north-south route through the city, in the early 1930s. There have been a few changes in the intervening years. The eighteenth-century shop, furthest right, was a victim of the Blitz. Other buildings have since changed use, notably the pair of early nineteenth-century houses beyond the St John's Lane junction (on the right), which have since been converted into a café and guest house. Further down on the left, the former Globe Public House and Cakebread Robey premises were demolished in the 1950s and 1970s respectively. In more recent years, Castle Street has ceased to be a thoroughfare and is blocked off at the bottom end to prevent traffic penetrating the pedestrianized city centre. Despite this, numerous vehicles ignore the no through road sign and continue to try.

St George's Street, the most prestigious section of Canterbury's main street (and part of the A2) decorated for Cricket Week in the early years of this century. This scene changed almost completely following the Baedeker Raid of 1 June 1942. As a result, only the gutted shell of St George's church (right) was left standing (see p. 79). Throughout the 1940s, the flattened area was the focus for planning disputes between those who wanted to rebuild piecemeal under private enterprise and those who preferred a collective approach using compulsory purchase. The street was finally redeveloped, initially under the auspices of the City Council, in the 1950s. Pedestrianization occurred in the 1970s. The forthcoming Whitefriars development scheme will see many of the 1950s buildings on the left swept away.

St George's Place at dawn on 1 June 1942. A once impressive row of late Georgian buildings has been reduced to gutted shells and smouldering rubble. Here, the fires caused by incendiary bombs burnt almost unchecked, the National Fire Service being too busy elsewhere. In the centre of the picture a fragmented shell is all that is left of Dr Wacher's house, one of the few properties which is still a private residence, rather than having been converted into offices. The area was earmarked for commercial use in the 1950s. New buildings such as the Kentish Gazette premises and the Martin Walter filling station were set back from the road, in anticipation of the widening of St George's Place to a dual carriageway which occurred in 1969. The Safeway store replaced the filling station and a car park in the 1980s.

Wincheap, a Canterbury suburb on the main A28 road to Ashford, in March 1955. An East Kent bus on a city service to Thannington passes beneath Wincheap 'number two' bridge, which is being prepared for demolition (the 'number one' bridge, adjacent to Canterbury East Station, survives today). The Elham Valley Line carried by this bridge had closed in 1947 after only sixty years of service. The railway embankments either side were dug out in the early 1960s and the soil used to form new embankments for the nearby ring road, the Rheims Way. Houses subsequently appeared in the gap to the left and a car park on the right. In the late 1960s, Cow Lane (right) was widened in advance of the construction of Wincheap Industrial Estate.

The choked High Street from the Guildhall Street junction in 1956. Bicycles, vans, a bus and a motorbike and side car are held up by parked delivery vans on both sides of the street. Later the same year, the relocation of the bus station from St Peter's Place to St George's Lane would reduce the number of buses in the main street. Then in the 1960s, the construction of the ring road would further ease the situation, albeit temporarily. Pedestrianization of The Parade, High Street and St Peter's Street finally came in the 1980s, at about the same time as the opening of the Canterbury bypass. Vehicular access is now only allowed to delivery lorries before half past ten and after four o'clock.

Union Street was one of the roads laid out in the early nineteenth century to provide housing for the families of soldiers stationed at the nearby barracks. From 1959 onwards, the area was subject to slum clearance. By October 1961, Union Street was in a transitional state, as pictured here. Houses on the north side (right) had been demolished and new council accommodation built. Moreover, the street itself had been considerably widened and become part of the A28 route to Thanet. It replaced the previous route in and out of the city via The Borough and Palace Street. The buildings on the south side, with the exception of the white-painted William IV Public House, would be pulled down in 1962 and blocks of flats constructed. Tourtel Road allowed the closure of Union street to through traffic in the late 1980's.

The Wincheap Green area seen from Station Road East in January 1963. Here Station Road meets Wincheap Street (left), Castle Street (far right) and Wincheap Green itself (right), as well as the station approach road. Within months, the area would be totally transformed by the construction of Wincheap Roundabout, part of the first stage of the ring road, which was opened in June 1963. All properties in the old picture were demolished. They are, from left to right: No. 1 Wincheap (empty by this time), the Georgian house known as The Cedars, (by this time the offices for British Road Services) and the Castle Hotel and Public House (see p. 52). Wincheap Roundabout has been altered in size a number of times in the intervening years.

This picture was taken to record a fire in the roof of the empty and derelict property at No. 2 Upper Bridge Street in March 1966. Beyond the fire engine is the St George's Crossroads (see front cover). By this time, details of the second stage of the ring road had been announced and all the old properties were destined for demolition to make way for St George's Roundabout. Greenfield's, far right, was one of a group of new shops built on a bomb site in the late 1950s to early 1960s and positioned to be compatible with the proposed road alterations. The second stage of the ring road was completed in late 1969.

An Austin 1100 and an Austin Cambridge plough their way through floodwater at the junction of Longport and Lower Chantry Lane in December 1967. Some eleven years earlier, Lower Chantry Lane (in the foreground) had been considerably widened to become part of the main road from Canterbury to Sandwich. The buildings of Canterbury Technical College loom up behind. Until 1937, the complex was the original Kent and Canterbury Hospital. New technical schools were built in the late 1960s, followed by the complete demolition of the old buildings in 1972. An attractive garden area laid out on the site has recently been lost beneath the new St Augustine Visitors' Centre (seen far left in the modern view). A roundabout now makes the junction a lot easier to negotiate.

A lone person negotiates the winding footpath along the Dane John Moat in May 1968, probably a route she has taken on countless shopping trips to the city centre. At this location, she passes an old ship's capstan and the weed-covered plinth upon which once stood a First World War tank before it was broken up for salvage in the last war. Only eighteen months later, this idyllic scene was destroyed forever. The trees were felled and the ground levelled prior to the construction of the second stage of the ring road from Wincheap Green to Broad Street. The capstan, once thought lost, is believed to be in a garden somewhere in the Whitstable area. Today, all that remains of the moat is a sterile green strip, brightened only by springtime daffodils.

The old A2 road from London passed through the ancient village of Harbledown on the last leg of its route to Canterbury. The road was narrow, hilly and winding. By the 1960s with vehicles, especially lorries, increasing in size, weight and quantity, the traffic situation became very difficult. Delays were common, accidents frequent and damage by vehicles to property was a regular occurrence. Relief finally came in the early 1970s with the building of Harbledown bypass. The old picture from May 1973 shows Dukes Meadow with surveyors' poles already in place. A group of councillors and road contractors walk the route of the proposed bypass just prior to its construction. The current view is taken from the footbridge over the bypass cutting.

Two
Entertainment and leisure

The County Athletic Grounds at the top end of Wincheap about a century ago. At this time the site was owned by John E. Wiltshier but rented and operated by haulier and sports enthusiast G.F. Finn. Before the First World War, the grounds were used for sports of all kinds, circuses, fêtes, hot air balloon demonstrations and early motor cycle events. After the First World War, the grounds became rather underused and run down, until being restored and taken over by Robert Brett & Sons. Their haulage premises were adjacent to the grounds. This situation lasted until as recently as 1996, when Brett's moved elsewhere and the whole site was sold for redevelopment. Today, Wincheap Park and Ride (see p. 96) and a Safeway superstore occupy the site.

St Lawrence Cricket Ground in the late Victorian period, with a number of finely dressed spectators enjoying a match despite a little light rain. Just beyond the marquee is the well known lime tree that actually stands on the playing area. The old view was taken before the construction of any of the ground's famous buildings, so familiar today. The wooden pavilion was erected in 1900 and its annexe was built nine years later. Both can be seen in the current picture. A large concrete stand was added in 1927. Today, St Lawrence Cricket Ground (also the Kent County headquarters) is enjoyed by many thousands of locals and visitors every season. Note that the current spectators' mode of dress is much more casual!

A boy from Simon Langton school dives into the cold, muddy waters of Canterbury Swimming Baths during an inter-school gala in the late 1930s. The open pool, situated off Whitehall Road, had been built in 1876 and used water channelled in directly from the adjacent River Stour. Quite understandably, it was only open during the summer months. Complete closure of the pool came just after the last war, due to health concerns. For many years afterwards, Canterbury had no public pool. Plans unveiled in April 1961 to build a new pool beside the Dane John Gardens did not come to fruition. Today's indoor heated bath at Kingsmead finally opened in 1970.

An illustration of the impressive symmetrical façade of the new Regal Cinema in subdued Art Deco style. It was taken from a souvenir booklet published to commemorate the Silver Jubilee of King George V in 1935. The well balanced proportions of the cinema frontage lasted only until October 1942, when a bomb destroyed the Regal ballroom to the right and part of the main cinema façade. A long queue waiting to see *Gone With the Wind* had a lucky escape. The surviving portion was subsequently repaired, the void to the right bricked off and the building re-opened, resulting in the somewhat lop-sided frontage seen today. The cinema, with much original decoration inside, is now called the Cannon.

Local residents enjoy the leafy surroundings of the Westgate or Tower Gardens on a hot summer's day in 1948. Some knit or read in the sunshine, while others doze off in the generous shade. These public gardens were once the private garden of Tower House (seen behind), which was the residence of the Williamson family who owned and ran the local tannery. The generous family gave both house and garden to the city in the 1930s. Tower House itself subsequently became the Mayor's Parlour. Note the square tower to the left, once part of the city wall defences. Today, the few local residents who still use Westgate Gardens are vastly outnumbered by hordes of schoolchildren, many of them visiting tourists.

Part of the Canterbury Festival Exhibition site in the Whitefriars area, shortly after its opening in June 1951. Canterbury was one of twenty cities chosen to stage the 1951 Festival of Britain and picked the history of Canterbury as its theme. In the foreground is a sculpture consisting of two moulded plaster hands, one carrying a sword, the other supporting a model of Lanfranc's Cathedral. This represented Canterbury's constant involvement in the struggles between church and state. Behind is a monastic herb garden against an ancient wall, once part of the Whitefriars Augustinian Friary (see p. 84). The site, including the old wall, was cleared to allow the post-war redevelopment of the area. Today it is a bleak loading area, which is itself due to be cleared and redeveloped shortly.

'Bat and trap' is a very old game which, as far as I can tell, is only played in the Canterbury area of Kent. The old picture from 1954 shows a game being played in the rear garden of the White Hart public house in Worthgate Place. The size of the crowd and the fact that the featured player, Teddy Long, is wearing his Sunday best is probably due to the presence of a BBC Newsreel team. Sadly, there is insufficient space here to explain the curious rules of the game. It will suffice to say that it is a competitive team game played almost exclusively in pub gardens. The current picture shows a smaller, informal and more typical gathering at The Swan in Sturry, on a warm summer's evening in 1997.

A happy crowd willingly smile for the cameraman as they wait for the 1954 carnival to begin. They are standing alongside the perimeter wall of Thannington Pumping Station. Family groups, including many senior members, predominate. Practically all of the May family can be seen to the right. This was indeed the golden age of the annual carnival. Sadly, in recent years this tradition has seen a significant decline in both spectators and participants, which has been blamed largely on television. In 1997 a local Canterbury paper, the *Kentish Gazette*, actively championed the carnival and tried to boost its popularity. It met with partial success, as the current picture testifies. Are the older family members at home checking their lottery numbers?

These five serious young men, pictured in March 1965, comprise The Wilde Flowers, one of the more adventurous and pioneering semi-professional bands in 1960s Canterbury. They are, left to right: Hugh Hopper, Richard Sinclair, Brian Hopper, Kevin Ayres and Robert Wyatt. This line-up later spawned two further bands, The Soft Machine and Caravan, that went on to achieve national and even international success. More importantly, they developed the 'Canterbury Sound' or 'Style, a genre recognized across the world today. It is best described as an eccentric form of jazz-rock characterized by constantly shifting time signatures and chord changes. Today, only Hugh Hopper can be regularly seen in Canterbury. He still performs at gigs across Europe and records an average two or three CDs a year!

The sad sight of the original Marlowe Theatre in St Margaret's Street being demolished in June 1982, to make way for a shopping development. The theatre had been converted from an old cinema and opened in 1951. Many famous personalities and bands have appeared here over the years, notably Pink Floyd in March 1969. The new Marlowe Theatre found a home in another redundant cinema, The Odeon in The Friars, which was extensively altered for the purpose. Fortunately, the cinema's splendid early 1930s Art Deco façade was retained and can be seen in the current view. Also note the Victorian Marlowe Memorial, a semi-naked muse on her stone plinth in the foreground, latterly moved from the Dane John Gardens.

Three
Secondary streets

Many old timber framed buildings characterize pre-war Burgate Street, which runs parallel to the main thoroughfares of St George's Street and The Parade. Dominating the old picture are the premises of Philpot's Cooperage at No. 50 Burgate Street, here seen in the 1880s. It is an early seventeenth-century double-jettied and gabled structure, a typical vernacular design of the period. The building, as well as those either side, was completely destroyed in the main Blitz of 1 June 1942.

The well known Buttermarket at the end of the last century. Three of Canterbury's secondary streets converge here, namely Burgate Street, Mercery Lane and Sun Street. The famous Marlowe Memorial, erected here in 1891, dominates the scene (see p. 30). Soaring up behind is the battered and weathered Christ Church Gate, the main entrance to Canterbury Cathedral. In 1921, the Marlowe Memorial was moved to Dane John, to make way for the city's First World War memorial. This can be seen in the current view. The gateway was restored in stages during the 1930s. The Buttermarket has seen many changes this century, even becoming a car park in the 1950s! Today it is crowded with tourists, many of whom enjoy the hospitality of the Olive Branch Public House, whose tables and umbrellas occupy much of the area.

Lady Wootton's Green in the 1890s, looking towards the city wall and Cathedral beyond. Originally, the lane led directly to Findon Gate and St Augustine's Abbey, behind the camera (see p. 35). To the left is a delightful pair of seventeenth-century cottages, outside which an elderly woman is cleaning the footpath. Further down is a short terrace of eighteenth-century houses fronting Broad Street and standing between the two branches of Lady Wootton's Green. In the 1920s, the eighteenth-century terrace was demolished and a small formal garden created between the two branches of the road. The pair of seventeenth-century cottages were pulled down following war damage in 1942. The neo-Georgian terrace seen today was constructed in the 1950s.

King Street runs in a north-south direction parallel to the main shopping thoroughfare of Palace Street for much of its length. Unlike its grander neighbour, it has always been mostly residential and used by traffic gaining access to the adjacent lanes. The old picture from 1938 shows Nos 24 to 27 intact and the remains of No. 23, following the clearance of much of Knotts Lane to the left. These King Street properties were empty by 1940 and demolished in 1946. Public conveniences were built on the site in the 1950s. Plans to widen King Street, as part of a north-south relief road, were not taken up and it remains a narrow residential street today.

The Findon Gate in Monastery Street, seen from Lady Wootton's Green, a few days after the main air raid of 1 June 1942. Although not actually hit, the old gateway, once the main access to St Augustine's Abbey, was badly damaged by the blast. There was so much damage to the stone facing of its northern (left hand) tower that the structure had to be shored up until after the war. Restoration and repair took place in 1947, although the stone used in this process has not weathered well, as the current picture testifies. Comparison of the two views also shows the changes that have occurred to the small formal garden area between the two branches of Lady Wootton's Green (see p. 33).

Archaeologist Mr Sheppard Frere (left) oversees the mechanical clearance of a large bomb site, between Iron Bar Lane and Canterbury Lane, in the summer of 1949. Designated 'Area R', the site subsequently yielded a small sixteenth-century cellar and the junction of two Roman city roads. Parked cars and a blitzed garage in the narrow Iron Bar Lane can be seen beyond the tree saplings and buddleia (see p. 58). Post-war redevelopment of the area began in 1952, with the widening of Iron Bar Lane and the creation of Link Lane. The latter was designed to link a new loading area in Iron Bar Lane to the parallel Canterbury Lane. The utilitarian modern shops seen in the current view were erected in the late 1950s.

St Radigund's Street in 1957, a quiet residential road in the north of the city. In medieval times it ran along the inside of the city wall. Many of its houses and buildings were constructed following the demolition of the wall here in the late eighteenth and early nineteenth centuries. Post-war plans for Canterbury were destined to change St Radigund's Street greatly. It was to become a dual carriageway and part of the city's ring road. Much advance demolition took place throughout the 1960s and early 1970s and temporary car parks occupied the voids between the few surviving buildings. The third stage of the ring road was cancelled in 1975. Subsequent residential development has returned the street to something like its 1950s appearance.

The old view, from September 1960, was taken at the top end of Stour Street, opposite the tannery. It shows two old buildings soon to be pulled down. The seventeenth-century jettied house was replaced by the Rosemary Lane car park and the early nineteenth-century brick house made way for an extension to the gardens of the nearby almshouse. Early 1970s plans to turn Stour Street into a wide access road to a proposed lorry unloading area were thankfully dropped. Current plans have once again earmarked the sites of both lost houses for residential development. Ironically, this will mean the destruction of the surviving ground floor wall of the early nineteenth-century house that currently survives as a boundary to the garden behind. It can be seen in the current view.

The 'Red Dean' of Canterbury Cathedral, Hewlett Johnson, holds a CND banner as he leads a good-natured protest march out of Rose Lane, across Watling Street and on to the City Council offices at the Dane John in February 1960. While the marchers are the photographer's intended subject, the buildings on either side of the narrow Rose Lane junction are of equal interest. The typewriter shop (right) was demolished in 1961 and the grocer's shop (left) in 1962. Rose Lane was widened afterwards to serve the proposed Civic Centre on the site of Watling Street car park, a development that never materialized. All the 1960s buildings seen to the right in the current view are due to be demolished as part of the Whitefriars development scheme.

A lovely terrace of four empty late eighteenth-century cottages in Nackington Road in 1964, seen from the rear access road to the Kent and Canterbury Hospital. A woman with a pram has stopped to survey the end cottage, as if to pay her last respects prior to its demolition. New development is creeping in from the right. That particular new house is being built on top of the former Elham Valley railway line embankment. The railway bridge over Nackington Road had only recently been removed. The old cottages were soon replaced by further new semi-detached houses set back from the road, as seen in the current photograph.

A mid-1960s view of the south side of Dover Street, seen from near its junction with Upper Bridge Street. The filling station and garage of Bligh Bros Ltd dominates the picture. The complex, completed in 1960, had replaced a smaller garage and a row of ancient cottages on the same site. The new garage was destined to have a very short life, being demolished in the mid 1970s for an office development that never appeared. Beyond and set well back is the Nags Head public house, opened in 1958. It is now a wine bar, working its way through an ever changing succession of names. Fortunately, the cottages furthest from the camera have altered very little in the intervening years.

The once grand and prestigious town houses of Station Road East in June 1978. By this time, they had been blighted by the busy ring road immediately behind and an intrusive footbridge over it. Construction of the latter necessitated the demolition of one of the houses, thus bisecting the terrace. Station Road East had been created in 1860 to serve the new station of the London, Chatham and Dover Railway. The houses were built in the last quarter of the nineteenth century. Piecemeal demolition of empty properties had already begun in 1978, a sure way to hasten the departure of those occupants who remained. The cleared site remained empty until the early 1990s, when the current development of offices and flats emerged.

Four
Pubs and hotels

The George and Dragon inn, a superb three-storey timber framed structure on the north side of the High Street, from a pictorial survey of Canterbury undertaken in the 1880s. It appears to be of late sixteenth- or early seventeenth-century date and was probably built as two separate properties, hence the staggered jetty at second floor level. Mathematical tiles and probably the bay windows were added in the eighteenth century, a partial attempt to 'Georgianize' the structure. To the left is the nineteenth-century Greyhound public house. Both buildings featured here were demolished in 1897 to make way for the Beaney Institute, an overblown late Victorian pastiche, described as 'ludicrous' in the highly regarded 1970 book *Canterbury: City Buildings series*.

The Farriers Arms public house on the west side of King Street in about 1930. Built in the late seventeenth century, it originally had nine smaller early Georgian sash windows on the front elevation, including the one above the door. In around 1800, the four larger Regency windows seen in the old view were substituted. The pub closed around the time the older picture was taken and the building became a private dwelling. In the 1960s, many ancient houses in King Street were demolished and replaced by new developments, some slightly more memorable than others. The former Farriers Arms was luckier than most. It received a preservation order in 1966 and was restored by Anthony Swaine (see p. 74), who replaced the original early Georgian window pattern.

From the turn of the century until the mid 1930s, a number of Canterbury public houses were completely rebuilt. An early example of this was the Three Compasses on the north side of St Peter's Street. The old photograph shows the original pub building as it was in 1886. It is a mid seventeenth-century timber-framed structure with two jetties and one huge gable, very similar to the oldest part of Slatters Hotel, still standing in St Margaret's street today. The old Three Compasses was demolished in 1903 and its more fanciful replacement immediately built. The shop to its right has also since been completely rebuilt.

The Baker's Temperance Hotel, on the corner of St George's Street and Rose Lane, at the turn of the century. Not long before this picture was taken, the mainly seventeenth-century building had dummy Tudor-style timbers applied to its rendered façade. The genuine timbers of its structural framing were buried beneath the plaster work. Baker's Hotel transferred to a former private house in Ivy Lane during the mid-1930s and its old premises were adapted to become the Parade Chambers. This was a collection of offices, small businesses and tea rooms, all housed under the same roof. Parade Chambers was completely destroyed in the main Blitz of 1 June 1942. Ten years later, Rose Lane (right) was widened across the site of the lost building and its rubble was used to fill cellars now hidden beneath the roadway.

St Dunstan's Street contains a wealth of lovely old timber-framed buildings, the best of which are the group on its south side. These three-storey double-jettied and multi-gabled structures date from the sixteenth and seventeenth centuries and include the famous House of Agnes inn. Another part contains a public house known in the 1940s as the Rose and Crown. The old picture shows the affect of blast damage from a bomb that destroyed properties at the Station Road West junction opposite in June 1942. Fortunately, the damage was subsequently repaired and the pub re-opened. Today, it has fallen victim to the current fad for changing pub names and is now called the Tap and Spile!

There was no debate as to whether or not to save the Royal Fountain hotel in St Margaret's Street following the Blitz, because it was utterly destroyed by firebombs in the early hours of 1 June 1942. The old photograph, taken a few days later, shows members of the armed forces clearing the debris of this once grand building. The hotel was neither rebuilt nor re-opened elsewhere. In the early post-war years, archaeologists dug in its complex of cellars, before they were filled in and a car park laid out. Plans for the cross-city relief road to cross here protected the site from redevelopment until the scheme was dropped in the late 1960s. Nevertheless, it was nearly twenty years before the present shopping development was built.

'No more wallop' was the caption beneath this picture when it first appeared in the *Kentish Gazette* in January 1955. It shows the last moments of the Riding Gate public house at the top end of Watling Street. Originally built in the early nineteenth century, the pub was named after the adjacent city gate, long since gone. It was being demolished to make way for Riding Gate roundabout. This was not being built for the ring road (although it was on the proposed route), but in preparation for the opening of the new bus station in nearby St George's Lane. Many of Canterbury's pubs were situated at corners or junctions, so a number fell victim to post-war road improvement schemes.

The High Street lost some noted historic buildings in the 1950s. Amongst these was the famous Fleur de Lis hotel, pictured here in 1955 when its future was in serious doubt. On the surface is an eighteenth-century façade, largely of mathematical tiles, but beneath was an ancient structure with some sections dating back to the fourteenth century. The interior contained some superb wood panelling and an exquisite staircase, while the rear elevation displayed a jumble of timbered elevations and roof profiles. The hotel was offered for sale in the mid-1950s and changed hands several times. Eventually, demolition was proposed and conservationists lobbied for its retention. Sadly, much of its interior was plundered for private re-use and the whole structure was pulled down in March 1958.

The Man of Kent public house, on the corner of Worthgate Place and Pin Hill (right), in 1965. This interesting building, constructed in two distinct periods, dates from the seventeenth century and has a nineteenth-century slate-roofed pub extension. It was threatened with demolition for the second stage of the ring road, in the course of which Pin Hill would become a dual carriageway. In the event, only the nineteenth-century addition was pulled down, the original part later reverting to a house. With the general decline in the number of city pubs in the 1960s, those lost to road schemes were not replaced. However, the name 'Man of Kent' transferred to the nearby Station Hotel. Sadly, at the time of writing, it has again been renamed The Roundhouse and the old pub name is now lost once more.

The character and style of Canterbury pubs has changed radically in recent years, as these pictures clearly testify. The old photograph from December 1962 shows William and Ethel Lack, licensees of the Castle Hotel, unhappy at the imminent forced closure of their premises. Its demolition was needed for the construction of Wincheap roundabout (see p. 16). Note the hand pumps, doilies, numerous spirit bottles and the ubiquitous pile of pennies on the bar. Today, the decline in the popularity of pubs has been halted by the opening of a number of large licensed premises, some themed, with an emphasis on attracting younger adults. One of these is Churchill's Café Bar in St George's Place, opened in November 1996. Pictured here, in the upstairs Bridge Bar, is bar tender Paul Schofield and daytime manageress Lesley Kennedy.

Five

Lanes, rows and squares

Ivy Lane, taken from a watercolour painted at the turn of the century. The row of ancient tottering cottages depicted here stretches right down to the Lower Chantry Lane junction. They include two fourteenth-century Wealden-type houses, long since divided into tenements. Cottages at the far end were subject to slum clearance in the 1920s, while others were damaged in the Blitz in 1942. One of the Wealden houses was demolished in about 1915 and replaced by a row of brick cottages. The other was renovated, but only finally saved from slum clearance in the late 1950s.

Knotts Lane, a minor thoroughfare of very
humble dwellings, in the early 1930s when the
whole area was being considered for slum
clearance. This was as a direct result of the
setting up of the City Council Housing
Committee in 1925 and the establishment of
new council housing estates on the city outskirts
over the following ten years. The ancient
houses, dominated by the three storey double-
jettied and gabled seventeenth-century house at
No. 22 (left), were mostly taken down in 1937
and 1938. The cleared site became a scrapyard
on the west (left) side and a car park on the east.
The area again underwent residential
redevelopment from the early 1970s onwards.

Right up to the late 1930s, small corners in the very heart of Canterbury were still crowded with tiny cottages. Amongst them were the late eighteenth-century houses of Rose Square, just off Rose Lane and near to the main shopping thoroughfare of St George's Street. The old view dates from 1930, when some of the cottages, just off left, had been demolished to make way for a narrow rear entrance to the new Marks and Spencer store in St George's Street. All the houses had gone by 1939, allowing Marks and Spencer to enlarge the rear of their shop. A further massive rear extension in the early 1970s covered the entire former Rose Square area, hence the current view.

The mostly seventeenth-century cottages of Old Ruttington Lane, seen from the junction with Broad Street, in the early 1930s. Many of these small dwellings were well constructed and did not feature in the slum clearance programmes of the 1920s and 1930s. Number 55, the home of Alice Blackman, was entirely brick built and carried a date stone of 1688. Sadly, the Blitz ravaged the lane and Granny Blackman lost her little house. In the early post-war years, prefabricated school buildings were erected on the site of the lost cottages. They are still there today, hidden here by the dense foliage of self-sown trees. The building in the foreground (right) also replaced its blitzed predecessor.

Three early eighteenth-century cottages at Nos 62, 64 and 66 St Peter's Lane, in about 1935, having just been identified as part of 'Slum Clearance Area No. 11'. As with most of the ancient dwellings in this lane, they were of very cheap construction, being made of brick only in the lower storey of the front elevation. The remainder would have been poor timber framing hidden by weather boarding, tiles or in this case, pebble dashing. Houses on the east side of the lane, including these, backed onto a common yard containing the privies, washing lines and a huge iron mangle. The cottages were demolished in 1937 and the site remained empty until the early post-war years. Then prefabricated college buildings were erected here. They remain today.

Iron Bar Lane is the third of five parallel lanes that run between the main thoroughfare of St George's Street and the secondary Burgate Street. The lane was all but flattened in the Blitz of 1 June 1942. The old picture from April 1949 shows an archaeological dig in the cellar and rear garden of No. 19 St George's Street, which once stood on the junction with Iron Bar Lane. Before the Blitz, the lane started as a non-vehicular passage running through No. 19 to one side and beneath its upper storey. The 1952 remodelling of Iron Bar Lane has kept the St George's Street end as a foot passage, but widened the Burgate end to provide access to the new service area and Link Lane (see p. 36).

Westgate Grove is a pedestrian thoroughfare but a dead end for vehicles, leaving St Dunstan's Street near the Westgate and parallel to the River Stour. The medieval and early post-medieval buildings on its west side are pictured here from the adjacent Westgate Gardens in the late 1940s. The houses once on its east side had been demolished at least a hundred years before. Because of the quaintness of its cottages, pre-war slum clearance had never been considered. Westgate Grove also escaped bomb damage. Not so lucky was Kennett's Depository, at the far end of the old view, which had been truncated in 1942 and completely demolished by 1950. Today, Westgate Grove attracts tourists, many taking a river tour at the same time.

Originally Whitehorse Lane was called
Monetaria, for the City Mint was located here.
The old photograph, from September 1960,
shows the east side of the lane with seventeenth-
and eighteenth-century houses, as well as a
nineteenth-century warehouse, built near the
site of the mint. The post-war road plan
identified Whitehorse Lane as a main traffic
thoroughfare linking the High Street (furthest
from the camera) to the proposed cross-city relief
road. This would result in a much wider road.
Consequently, from the early 1960s onwards,
many of its ancient dwellings were pulled down.
Such plans have long since been cancelled and
this somewhat run down area is awaiting
redevelopment for shopping, but a date for this
work has yet to be fixed.

The early nineteenth-century terrace on the north side of Simmonds Row, consisting of eight cottages, in 1960. A matching terrace on the south side had been demolished in the early 1950s and replaced by a row of lock-up garages. The motor cycle shop at the junction in the foreground was gutted by fire in 1962. It remained derelict until its demolition, together with all the surviving houses of Simmonds Row, in around 1968. In the early 1970s, the Wincheap Industrial Estate was established on the adjacent former allotments and orchards. Simmonds Row became the start of the estate's main access road. It was widened as a result and renamed Simmonds Road.

The lanes that cross the Whitefriars area of Canterbury have undergone drastic changes in the last forty years. Although the Blitz accounted for some losses, the essential character of these lanes remained unaltered until demolition and road widening commenced in the early 1960s. One such tiny lane was Gravel Walk. The old view from February 1963 was taken from the lane and looks into the Victorian burial ground associated with St Mary Bredin Church. The area was bulldozed in 1965 and became a temporary car park. As far as I can ascertain, the actual burials remained in situ. The multi-storey car park was built across here in 1969. It is due to be demolished itself in the next few years and the area redeveloped yet again, this time for shopping.

Mill Lane, seen from across King Street, in 1964. The cottages at Nos 19 to 21 date from the second quarter of the nineteenth century. Other houses on the corner site had been demolished some time before. During the year this picture was taken, the Blackfriars area of Canterbury, encompassing Blackfriars Street, King Street and Mill Lane, was identified for slum clearance and redevelopment. However, by this time, local conservationists had found a voice and protests were lodged. Sadly, many of the old houses, including these in Mill Lane, came down in 1966 despite protests. A neo-Georgian housing development appeared across much of the site in the late 1960s, dubbed a 'miniature Chelsea' by its critics.

In 1973, local government reorganization robbed Canterbury of its County Borough status. The resulting new City Council included a conservation department for the first time and appreciation for the retention of old buildings was officially recognized. Unfortunately, this had come too late for certain buildings already condemned. The old picture from November 1974 shows Union Row, off Ivy Lane, derelict and mostly stripped out prior to demolition. To the left is the premises of Amey & Son Ltd, also doomed. Another new phenomenon of the early 1970s was squatting and these cottages were amongst those occupied as a protest against empty properties. Sadly, the houses and Amey's were pulled down during the following year and Longport Coach Park was expanded (see p. 94).

Six
Shops and businesses

Right up to the Blitz, F.W. Martin, draper, silk merchant, costumier and ladies' outfitter, traded from large premises at Nos 1 and 2 St George's Street. The old photograph shows a beautiful Martin's window display from the 1920s. How much would this collection of dresses, furs and cloche hats be worth today? Their shop was destroyed in the Baedeker Raid of 1 June 1942. Later, Martin's re-opened in St Margaret's Street. In 1957, a new Co-operative store was built on the site of the blitzed Martin's shop. Then, in the mid 1980s, C & A took over from the Co-op and a clothing store could once more be found on the site.

The men, horses and wagons of coal merchants Pilch, Collard & Co. Ltd line up for the camera at their depot in Gordon Road, adjacent to the East Station's railway coal yard. The domestic coal business was at its peak in the 1890s. The firm traded in coal from all over the British Isles and from the 1920s onwards also operated from Chislet Colliery in the Kent coal field. In 1968, the firm was bought up by Jack and Edie Lee. In the early 1980s, they relocated to Chartham. In April 1996, their son Barry Lee sold up to major coal merchants Corralls. The current picture, taken in the Chartham yard, shows Gordon Southfield (left) and Jim Hurst (right) by their coal lorries.

The old view is typical of a posed photograph of a butcher's shop, taken in the late Victorian or Edwardian periods. Here, the proud butcher, Henry Cornes, stands in the doorway of his shop at No. 14 Mercery Lane, surrounded by carcasses. In the normal course of events, much of the meat would be stored inside but some, especially rabbits and game, would still be displayed outside at the mercy of the elements and of bluebottles. Today, butchers' shops give freshness and hygiene much more importance. One of the best in Canterbury is Wincheap Butchers, run by father and son team Jim and Richard Williams for the last eighteen years. In the current view, Richard stands outside their premises at No. 26 Wincheap.

In 1930s Canterbury, shops constructed in the new International Modern style were few and far between. One of the best was the new Barrett's shop in St Peter's Street. It is pictured here shortly after opening on 18 March 1938. Only four months before, their previous shop on the site had been burnt out. Designed by architect H. Campbell Ashenden, the façade was finished in bronze and Roman marble and the central arcade allowed a generous window display area. Sadly, the new shop was itself badly damaged by fire in a late wartime raid on 22 January 1944. What was left of it hung on until the late 1970s, when Barrett's built new premises here. They were not allowed to use a modern style, the City Council preferring the use of vernacular pastiche.

In the 1940's, building societies did not enjoy the high profile they have today. The premises of societies in Canterbury, such as the Isle of Thanet, Temperance Permanent and Halifax, were all in St George's Place, within converted Georgian houses and well away from the main shopping area. The office for the Halifax, at No. 34 St George's Place, is pictured here in the late 1940s. Note the wonderful 'between the wars' frontage, sadly since destroyed. Today, the building societies have virtually taken over the main shopping streets in many towns. Most are now banks and many of the old names have disappeared in mergers. The current picture shows the prominent Halifax premises in St George's Lane, complete with cash dispensing machines.

In late 1940s Canterbury, the main street contained a miscellany of useful small shops. One did not have to go far to find a grocer, butcher, greengrocer or baker. The old picture features Nos 12 to 14 High Street, being (right to left) Curry's Cycles and Radios, Maypole Dairy Co. and the grocer Lipton's. So why did all these small traders either disappear or move out of town? There are many reasons, including the rapid rise of rates and rents, the exclusion of private cars from the city centre and the inability of small local firms to compete with the incoming chains. Today's traders in Nos 12 to 14 are Woolwich Building Society and a computer software shop.

LIPTON

Lipton's the grocers at No. 14 High Street, in June 1946, also featured on the previous page. The window contains a neat display of tinned and packed food, including the famous Lipton's Tea. At this time, shopping was done by housewives, who mainly travelled into town on the bus, often on a daily basis. From the late 1950s onwards, medium-sized supermarkets such as Victor Value and Pricerite emerged, but were still located in the city centre. Today, lifestyle changes, with both partners working, means weekly shopping by car at large out-of-town hypermarkets. Pictured here is the entrance to Safeway in Wincheap, where all foodstuffs can be purchased under one roof.

The old view from 1955 shows the prefabricated shops on the Longmarket site, shortly after Mr R.E. Cranfield had set up the Camera Shop (left). He had come to Canterbury in 1953 and for two years ran a professional studio at No. 8 High Street. In 1959, the Longmarket site was cleared prior to redevelopment (see p. 86). The Camera Shop was the last prefab left standing as Mr Cranfield could not find new premises. Fortunately, he was eventually able to move into a former sweet shop at No. 43 Burgate. As his business expanded, Cranfield took over two local firms, namely Fisk-Moore and Photocentre, then opened a hi-fi shop also in Burgate and an optical shop in Butchery Lane. In more recent years, extortionate rents and the recession mean that Cranfield's now has only one camera shop once again. In 1997, Mr Cranfield's daughter Sarah took over the business. Both are pictured here outside the Burgate premises.

In the early 1950s, there were five local papers published in Canterbury, namely the *Kent Messenger*, *Kent Herald*, *Kentish Express*, *Kentish Observer* and *Kentish Gazette*. The old picture was taken in the printing works of the *Kentish Gazette* in St George's Street. An editorial secretary watches the type-setter create lines of type in hot metal, to be locked into pages for printing on the press behind. Today, the *Gazette* is part of the Messenger Group and published, together with its sister paper *The Extra*, in premises in St George's Place (opened in 1954). The current view features Editorial Secretary Sarah Bailey, with Chief Sub-Editor Roger Mapstone, who is typing up copy to be sent to Larkfield to be printed. All the other local papers mentioned above are no longer published.

A fine portrait of Anthony Swaine FRIBA FSA FASI, taken during December 1965, at his office in Latchmere House, Watling Street. By this time, he had been in business for twenty years. Prior to 1945, Tony worked for the Dean and Chapter. During the Blitz, when he was a war damage assessor in the city, it became apparent to him that many of the damaged buildings pulled down by the local authorities could easily have been saved. A keen conservationist, he was one of the lone voices in the 1950s and 1960s appalled at the loss of so many historic buildings to the bulldozer. He restored a number of saved buildings including Eastbridge Hospital and Hall Place in Ivy Lane. Now well into his eighties, Tony still works full time!

Seven
Significant lost buildings

The lofty symmetrical frontage of the Countess of Huntingdon church, an offshoot of the Congregational faith, designed by W.F. Poulton and built in 1863. Situated on the north side of Watling Street, it is pictured here around 1910, when the Minister was the Revd Alex Snape. Sadly, the church was gutted in a minor air raid during June 1942 and the shell was destroyed in the infamous daylight raid of 31 October the same year. In the late 1940s, a prefabricated church was erected here. An impressive permanent replacement was constructed adjacent to the same site in the mid-1950s. Unfortunately, the new church is due to be swept away in the Whitefriars redevelopment scheme and yet another version built on the opposite side of the road.

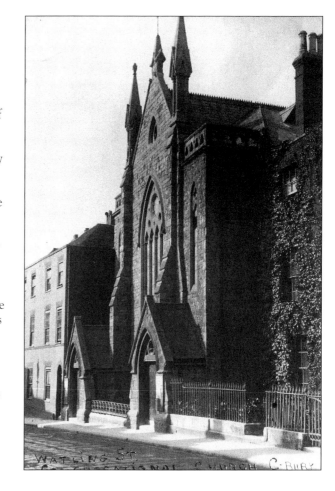

Dominating the city skyline, second only to the Cathedral, was Abbotts Mill, seen from St Radigund's Street in the early 1920s. This six storey timber-framed structure was designed by John Smeaton (also responsible for the Eddystone Lighthouse) and built in 1792. In the 1880s, the mill was owned by famous Canterbury artist Thomas Sidney Cooper, together with the nearby Westgate Mill (see p. 83). The mill was utterly destroyed in a spectacular and memorable blaze on 17 October 1933. The site has been empty ever since and today is a popular beer garden associated with the nearby Millers Arms public house. Stone and iron fragments from the lost mill can still be found on the site.

The Priory was a seventeenth-century L-shaped house that stood on the northern corner of Broad Street at its junction with Lady Wootton's Green. The old picture dates from 1910. The timber-framed jettied upper storey is clad in mathematical tiles to imitate brick, whilst the lower storey is built in brick and Caen stone blocks. The stone, together with other architectural features, had been plundered from the ruins of nearby St Augustine's Abbey. The house was tidied up between the wars, losing much of its character in the process. Wartime incendiary bombs caused some fire damage to the structure, which gave sufficient justification to the authorities for the complete demolition of the Priory. Diocesan House, built in the typical Dean and Chapter neo-Georgian style, appeared on the site in 1955.

The central aisle of St Mary Bredin Church, looking towards the altar, in the early years of this century. Built in 1868, it replaced a smaller medieval church on the same site. The Victorian church was noted for its octagonal tower and spire, a prominent feature of pre-war cityscapes. The church was gutted in the main Blitz of June 1942 and demolished in the months that followed. The last traces of it finally disappeared in 1952, when Rose Lane alongside was considerably widened. A replacement church was built on a different site in 1957. The west ends of both medieval and Victorian churches were uncovered in an archaeological dig during 1980, prior to the construction of the Marlowe shopping arcade. The east end, where the altar once stood, has long since been buried beneath the modern carriageway, seen in the current view.

The shell of St George's Church in the main street. The old picture shows damage caused by incendiary bombs in the main Blitz of 1 June 1942, as well as by the local authority's attempt to pull down the entire remains. The demolition was halted by Canon Crum, who recognized the historical significance of the building (the lower part of the tower dates from the twelfth century). The shell lingered on until the early 1950s, with plans for its future swinging between its complete retention as a war memorial to its complete demolition for road widening and shopping space. In 1952, a compromise allowed the tower to remain, whilst the rest of the church, largely a Victorian rebuild, was swept away. The top of the tower, demolished in 1942, was rebuilt and the rest restored. Today it is a familiar Canterbury landmark.

The wonderful Regency Corn Exchange and Longmarket building was undoubtedly one of those blitz-damaged landmarks in Canterbury that could have been restored, had there been the will to do so. Despite some fire damage, the basic structure remained sound with little evidence of even a scorch mark on the beautiful St George's Street elevation. Nevertheless, most of the building was demolished during the second week of June 1942, a process just begun in the old picture. Prefabricated shops appeared on the site in 1947 (see p. 72) and a permanent modern replacement was built in 1960 (see p. 86). This in turn gave way to an over-scale pastiche development in the early 1990s, part of which is visible in the current view.

The Guildhall, similar in appearance to the old Corn Exchange, is seen here earlier this century. Its front High Street elevation of 1835 hid elements of a much older timber-framed medieval structure, with a Romanesque undercroft beneath. In the late 1940s, it became apparent that the remodelling of the Regency period paid more attention to aesthetics than to structural integrity. Imminent collapse was predicted. Consolidation and repair proposals were shunned in favour of demolition, a process that took place in stages between 1949 and 1955, despite an outcry from conservationists. The shoe shop built on the site in 1956 is featured in the current view. Parts of the Romanesque undercroft still exist in the shop's underground store room.

The ivy-clad shells of two brick Jacobean houses of 1625 on the north side of Watling Street. The old picture was taken in 1953, just prior to their demolition. Gutted by incendiary bombs in June 1942, recognition of their true historic worth prevented demolition at the time which was a remarkable achievement given the lack of concern for such factors elsewhere in the city. Far from being empty ruins, an office existed on the ground floor of No. 19 (right) beneath a temporary roof constructed within the shell. Following clearance, the site was used as a car park for nearly twenty years, until the present office development was constructed. The house to the right in both old and current views is the same age as the lost Jacobean houses.

Flames pour from the roof of Westgate Mill at The Causeway on the night of Tuesday 9 June 1954. Sadly, Canterbury's other water mills had met similar fates. Abbott's Mill was destroyed by fire in 1933 (see p. 76) and Barton Mill was badly damaged in 1951. The fire-damaged building, including sections only slightly affected, remained in position until demolition in 1958. The site remained empty for the next thirty-five years, during which time the mill races and some wall fragments could still be seen amid the undergrowth. In the last few years, a sheltered housing complex has been built on the site, part of which is a facsimile of the old water mill and can be seen in the current view.

Of the three friaries that once existed in Canterbury, substantial remains of two, namely the Greyfriars and Blackfriars, can still be found. Sadly, today nothing is left of the Whitefriars, who once had a significant walled friary off the south side of St George's Street. However, this has not always been the case, as the old picture clearly testifies. Dating from the mid 1960s, it shows a substantial wall, including blocked windows, that once formed part of a west range of buildings. Unbelievably, this wall was cleared away prior to the construction of the Whitefriars shopping development in 1970. Earlier, in 1951, other friary remains had been demolished prior to the development of the blitzed St George's Street (see p. 26), part of which is visible in both views.

Destruction of significant and much-loved Canterbury landmarks continued right up to the early 1970s. One of the last to perish was St Andrew's Presbyterian Church at Wincheap Green, pictured here just before demolition in 1973. Designed by city architect John Green Hall and built in red brick with stone dressing, this lovely church opened for worship in 1881. It became redundant in the mid 1960s and faced an uncertain future. It was demolished for a building scheme that never materialized. The derelict site, enclosed by hoardings, was still vacant twenty years later. During this time, closer inspection revealed that some of the church's basement walls still existed to a substantial height. The mixed development of housing and offices in the current view appeared in the early 1990s.

The modern Longmarket development of 1960, as seen from Rose Lane in March 1967. This had replaced prefabricated shops on the site (see p. 72), that had in turn been erected on the site of blitzed buildings, including the Corn Exchange (see p. 80). The 1960 scheme had been specially designed to allow unobstructed views of the Cathedral, as the old picture clearly illustrates. Unfortunately, the box-like appearance of this development, without much detail, meant that it earned few friends. The unloved buildings were demolished and replaced by a pastiche scheme that now obscures the Cathedral, as shown in the current view. Sadly, the vastly superior bank building of 1956, seen right, also perished recently, to be replaced by yet more pastiche, thus furthering the Disneyfication of Canterbury.

Eight
Transport

The famous old Invicta locomotive, photographed in 1906, on the day it was put on permanent display in the Dane John Moat. This venerable engine had been designed and built by George Stephenson for the Canterbury and Whitstable Railway, opened in 1830. However, it only operated over a short stretch of the line at the Whitstable end, the rest being controlled by stationary winding engines. By the late 1940s, the Invicta was in a very poor state and its disposal for scrap was considered. Fortunately, it was renovated instead and in 1969 it was moved to a new site on the other side of the city wall and later to a covered position in the new Canterbury Heritage Museum.

A Dennis lorry and trailer, owned by local hauliers C. & G. Yeoman, parked in their depot off Wincheap Grove in 1928. It is loaded with hop pockets, no doubt recently dried in one of the numerous oasts that existed in Canterbury at the time. The lorry had been purchased by Yeoman's as First World War surplus. Between the wars, early lorries worked alongside steam traction engines and local hauliers usually owned both. In 1949, Yeoman's were nationalized and their fleet taken over by British Road Services. The depot finally closed in the early 1980s and was replaced by a new Habitat store. Twice-weekly deliveries to the store are made by large modern lorries, often with trailers, as in the current view.

The Elham Valley Railway from Canterbury to Cheriton had a very short life. It opened in 1887 and closed in 1947 after only sixty years of operation. The line started at Harbledown Junction near Canterbury West Station and before very long came to Canterbury South Station, adjacent to the new Kent and Canterbury Hospital. The former station building is seen here, in the early 1950s, while being converted for use as a council house, a fate shared by Bridge Station (where my Uncle Bill lived for a while). The old station disappeared sometime in the late 1960s and part of the site was developed with bungalows. Recently, quality flats have appeared on the remainder of the site and are featured in the current picture.

Canterbury East Station approach, coal yard and goods sidings, as they were in September 1955. The picture was taken to record a derailment caused during shunting manoeuvres. Railway men can be seen inspecting the errant carriage. Numerous changes to the scene have occurred over the years. The dilapidated train shed, spanning the main line in the distance, was demolished and replaced by modern platform shelters in 1958. Railway freight traffic gradually transferred to the roads in the 1960s and 1970s as the motorway network took shape. The sidings saw less traffic and were lifted as they went out of use. Those on the right have now been replaced by the extended station car park, while those on the left have partially given way to a housing development.

The early post-war years saw an increase in bus travel, caused by various factors. These included the establishment of new out of town housing estates and schools, as well as the closure of some secondary railways. Bus design also underwent changes, not least of which was an increase in width and length. By the early 1950s, Canterbury's small bus station in St Peter's Place had become inadequate and many services operated from overflow positions in Station Road West. Consequently, a large new station was opened in St George's Lane during May 1956 and is pictured here during its first year. The heyday of bus travel was short lived, as the country moved towards universal car ownership. The current view shows fewer buses, as well as a dramatically different backdrop.

A lovely picture of North Lane Car Park in December 1958, not long after it had been expanded onto the site of demolished buildings. In the foreground can be seen a Ford Consul, a Standard Vanguard 10, Hillman Minx and an elderly Ford Anglia. The registration numbers would suggest that these vehicles were owned by local people. At this time, the limited number of tourists to the city usually arrived by train or coach. North Lane Car Park is still in use today, although its conversion into a riverside garden has been discussed. Vehicles parked here now often carry European plates and British-made cars are in the minority. Today, foreign tourists vie with local people for parking spaces.

Canterbury Fire Station, with its vehicles on parade, during a station open day in March 1957. Note that the all British line up still includes two Second World War utility vehicles (second and third from right). At this time, the station was along Old Dover Road and consisted of a converted farm house and corrugated iron sheds, built for the wartime National Fire Service in 1943. A new purpose-built fire station, opened in Upper Bridge Street in May 1967, can be seen in the current view. It would seem that at least some fire engines are now being imported from Europe after years of the fleet being dominated by British-made Dennis vehicles. The old fire station site is now a housing development and the old farm house has returned to residential use.

A wonderful panoramic view of Longport Coach Park, as it was in June 1961. The site is crowded with coaches exclusively from the home counties, including a number from the local B.E.T. companies of East Kent and Maidstone and District. At this time, the park could also be used by cars, not that there is any room for them on this day! By the mid 1970s, the first coaches from Europe had arrived. Consequently, the coach park was expanded by the demolition of the warehouse and terrace of houses behind (see p. 64). In the last few years, an extensive new coach park has been opened at Kingsmead. European coaches dominate, bringing an ever increasing number of tourists.

An unidentified 'N' class locomotive pauses at Canterbury West with a stopping train from Ashford to Margate in 1961, during the last year of steam operation on this line. Note that the 750 volt DC electric third rail is already in place. The central 'through' lines, a common practice of the South Eastern Railway, allowed freight trains or the occasional express to pass through the station, while a stopping train waited at the platform. With the decline in railway freight traffic, the central lines saw ever decreasing use and were finally lifted in January 1979. The current picture shows an electric multiple unit on a service bound for Thanet. Note that the scars of the sleepers for the through lines are still visible in the ballast.

Canterbury's post-war road plans encouraged the movement of cars into and through the city. Ultimately, four inner city multi-storey car parks were planned, but as an interim measure, vast amounts of surface car parking had to be provided. The old view shows acres of such temporary parking in Gravel Walk during the mid 1960s. Simon Langton School once stood on the site to the right. In the event, only one multi-storey was built, that on the south (left) side of Gravel Walk in 1969. Pedestrianization of the main street began in the 1970s. Sturry Road Park and Ride site opened at the end of the 1980s. A second site at Wincheap (featured in the current view) followed in 1994. Two more Park and Ride sites are planned in the near future.